HIDDEN Objects

This Book Belongs To:

_____

_____

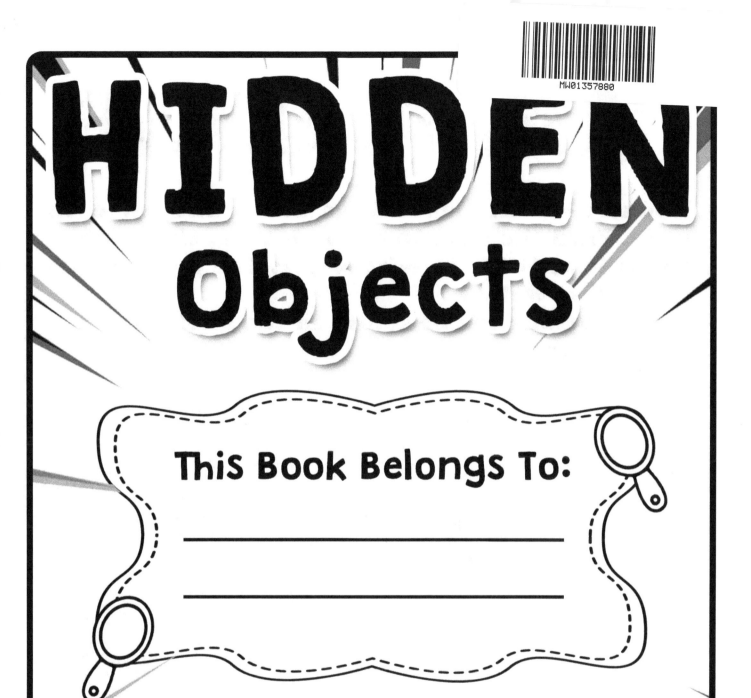

HOW TO SOLVE

About 6-12 hidden things are found on each page. Find the item in each picture, then either circle it or fill it in with color. The page can be colored as well.
The solutions can be found in the book's back.
Enjoy yourselves!

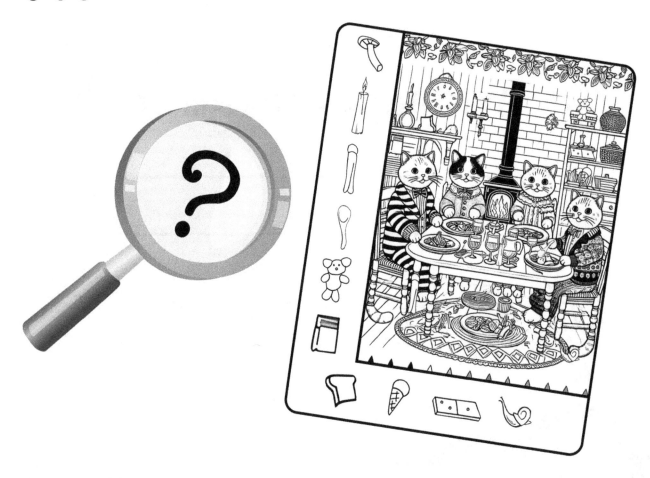

Look for every hidden item in the images!

COLOR TEST PAGE

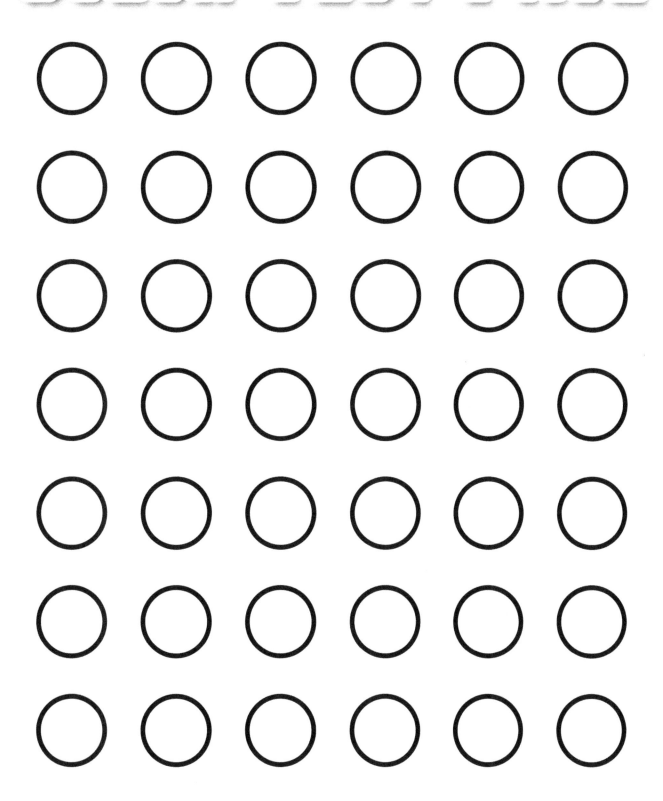

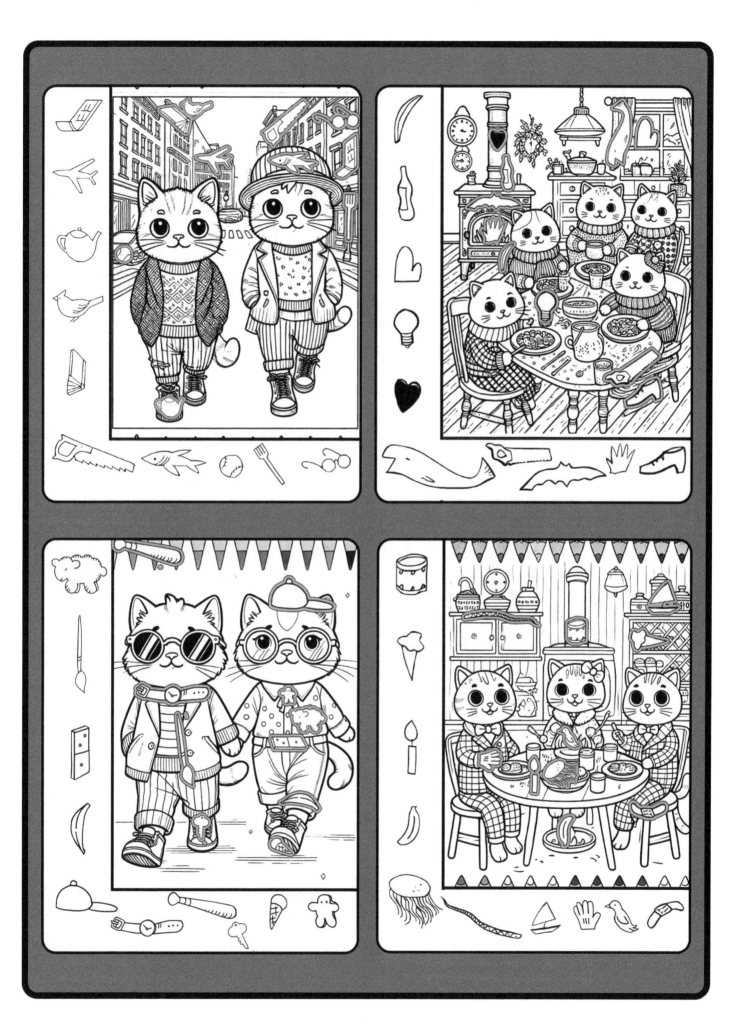

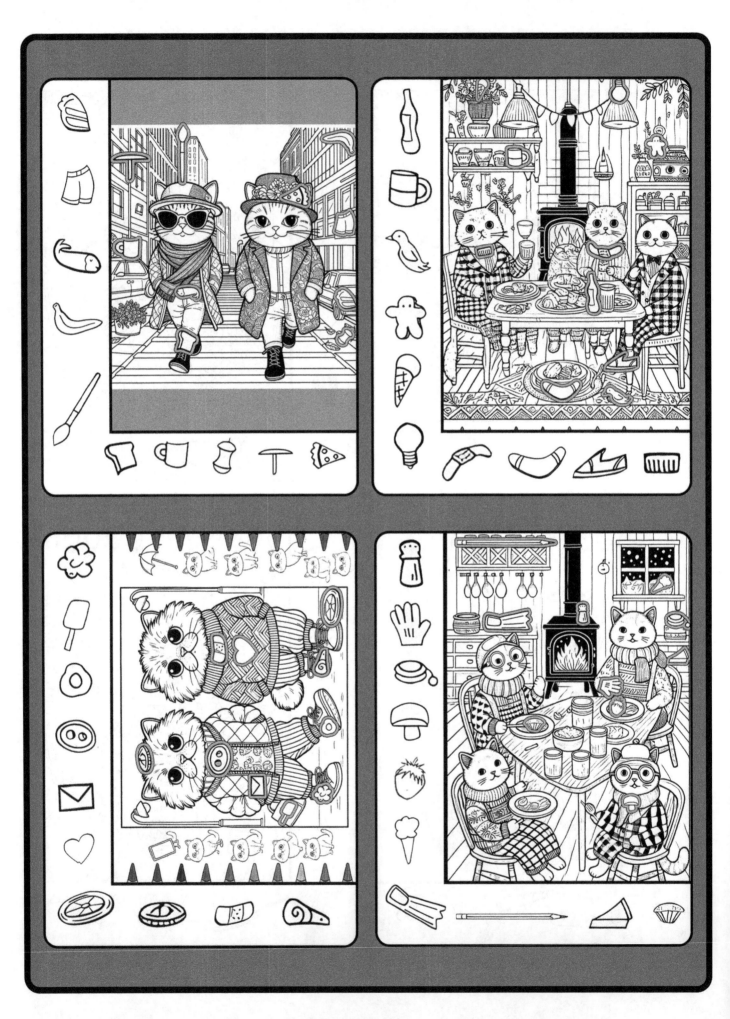